Is Our English Bible
Inspired?

Sam Gipp

DayStar Publishing
PO Box 464 • Miamitown, Ohio 45041

Is Our English Bible
Inspired?

Copyright, 2004
Dr. Samuel C. Gipp Th. D.

No part of this book may be reproduced either in printed form, electronically, or by any other means without the express written permission of the author. Said letter of permission must be displayed at the front of any electronically reproduced file.

(Think about it! You spend years writing a book and **thousands** of dollars to have it printed. You then rent warehouse space for them until they're sold. Then somebody puts it on the Internet and it gets copied free of charge. **It's not a question of getting rich!** If the books don't turn a profit, no more books can be written and all the books are rotting in some warehouse.)

2nd Printing 2010

ISBN 978-890120-43-6

Check out these Websites
samgipp.com
daystarpublishing.com

Printed by
Bible and Literature Missionary Foundation
713 Cannon Blvd., Shelbyville, TN 37160
(931) 684-0304 ● www.biblelit.org

Contents

1 Are You Afraid?..1

2 The Theories of Inspiration..5

3 We Stand on Two Legs...15

4 How Important Are the Originals?....................................27

5 Can a Translation Be Inspired?..33

6 Translations Vs the Originals...39

7 The "TR Man"...51

8 Can You Correct the Greek With the English?...............61

9 That Book in Your Hand...69

Preface

There is a battle raging right now over the Word of God. What is surprising is that some think this battle is new. Actually this battle began in the Garden of Eden when Satan posed the first doubt about the authority of the word of God when he asked, "Yes, hath God said?" No, the battle isn't new, it's just the battleground that changes. It was first fought in the Garden, and lost. Ezekiel 20:49 records that the inspiration of Scripture was being questioned in his time even as it was being written, "Then said I, Ah Lord GOD! they say of me, Doth he not speak parables?"

It was then fought in the institutions of higher education in Europe, and lost. In 1881 it was fought in the halls of Oxford and Cambridge, and lost. From there the battleground shifted to the United States. Harvard, Princeton and Yale, once great **Christian** institutions became the next battlegrounds and the next victims. After the surrender of the Ivy League schools the Methodists and Presbyterians fell. Next went the Southern Baptists universities. Finally, all that was left were the Independent Baptist and a handful of zealous Charismatics.

But, the persistent Questioner, always disguised as a "Believer," silently crept into the pulpits and classrooms of Fundamental churches and colleges and set the stage for the next edition of an age old battle. Now we are facing the battle within our ranks.

The battle plan is always the same.

1. The Adversary always presents himself as more "enlightened" than those who embrace the Bible.
2. He always offers a "different spin" on what the Lord said.
3. The Bible believer is made to look like an uneducated Hick if he maintains his "unenlightened" faith in God's word.
4. The Bible believer loses if he gives even one inch!

This book is written to help those "unenlightened" folks who believe the Bible is the **perfect** word of God and do not care what scholarship thinks of them. Every group before us gave in and bowed their knees to academia. It remains to be seen if we will join them or remain faithful to God and His word.

"Must everything in our world be predigested? Does the Bible have to be reduced to pablum? I refuse to believe that modern man, who has split the atom and is exploring space, is unable to cope with grandeur and glory of the King James Version"
                                                                       Winston Churchill

1
Are You Afraid?

A man who's afraid is not free. A man who is attached solely to the Bible enjoys the utmost freedom because his standard, the Bible, never changes and it expects no political concession from him. He is immune to the merciless opinion of Man.

All men like to give the impression that they are indeed free and in subjection to no one. That is why preachers are so quick to jump on the "King James" bandwagon. All they need to do is **say** they believe the Bible is perfect and they are automatically ascribed as possessing an independent spirit. There's only one problem. Not every one of them is truly free of fear. Many are intimidated by outside forces.

What Scares You?

For some it is the group they graduated from college with or those they work closely with. They fear that if they do not tow the old college line they will be ostracized. Thus, many preachers are more "cheerleaders" for the King James Bible than they are believers in it. They see the popularity of faith in God's Book and are not about to admit publicly the fears they have that it just might not be **absolutely** perfect. They seldom think deeply on the subject and instead are quick to praise it loud and boisterously. But they never really study the subject, relying instead on the consensus of the majority. Challenge their faith and, aware of their ignorance on the subject, they can only anathematize their opponents, hoping they will never really have to spend the study time needed to master the subject.

For others it is the fear of being inferior. They hold education as almost sacred and fear someone will think them uneducated if they don't agree with those whom they consider more educated than they. They will claim to believe the Bible if it advances their position but if academia says there are 20,000 errors in it then...**there are 20,000 errors in it!** After all, everyone knows scholars are never wrong. They're smarter than us. We make ourselves look like fools if we whoop and howl about the Bible being perfect if academia says it isn't.

The Problem

The problem arises when someone tries to please **both** groups. He wants preachers to believe that **he** believes the Bible is perfect but he fears the laughter of scholarship if he says a Book that they say has 20,000 errors has none. What's a man to do? Simple. He attempts to **redefine** what a "Bible believer" is. It is too "rural" and "backwoodsy" to claim the Book **in his hand** is without error so he attempts to push perfection back, back, back to the originals which he knows no one will ever obtain, thus assuring his "faith" cannot be disputed. Now all he has to do is to get all his "hick" friends to buy into his new definition of perfection and he's safe. But here is the rub!

Anyone can claim to believe in the inspiration of a Book (the Originals) which he has never seen nor ever will. This is what is known as "Coward's Faith" because the coward can bravely proclaim the inspiration and perfection of the Originals, knowing they have ceased to exist, hence they will never be examined and thus the coward's faith will never be challenged. But to put your faith in a Book **you can hold in your hand** is one of the bravest acts there is. When you say "That Book, that Book right there, that King James Bible is **perfect** and without error." you invite the ridicule (which a coward fears most) of friend and foe alike, and especially **academia**!

The Bottom Line

It really comes down to this; whose ridicule are you most afraid of, Bible believers' or scholars'? You cannot embrace both. One of these groups is going to pillar you. Which one's ire can you find acceptable and which one's ire sends shivers through you?

"The principles of all genuine liberty, and of wise laws and administrations are to be drawn from the Bible and sustained by its authority. The man therefore who weakens or destroys the divine authority of that book may be accessory to all the public disorders which society is doomed to suffer."
Noah Webster

2
The Theories of Inspiration

Men like to assign easily applied definitions to things to help them describe them. This is done concerning the definition of inspiration. There are six standard definitions that are universally applied to the method by which God inspired the Bible. To make it easy on the reader there is a "Yes" or "No" space in back of each definition. Read each definition and check "Yes" or "No" if you believe it best defines how our Bible was inspired.

1. Naturalistic Theory - This is the belief that **the Bible is not inspired by God** at all. It is no more than a collection of a mythological history of the world, a semi-accurate history of Israel and some admittedly wise sayings. This view is held by most scientists and is the one promoted and taught in every secular institute of "higher" education. Is this what you believe about inspiration? **Yes___ No___**

2. Neo-Orthodox Theory - This is the view that **God didn't inspire the Bible** but He uses it for His purposes, just as He might use the Koran or Book of Mormon or the words or writings of any other wise persons.

This is the view you will find in most modernistic churches, more interested in "world peace" than rectifying the wayward relationship of Man to his Creator. These folks **love** the "Sermon on the Mount" but pretend that Matthew 10:34, 35 are not in the Bible. They are quick to go to Scripture to justify their "world peace initiatives" but are blind to those which condemn them as sinners. This is why they can deny the perfection of Scripture and yet place Isaiah 2:4, "...and they shall beat their swords into plowshares," on the United Nations building and never feel hypocritical. They figure, the Bible isn't **really** inspired but it sure helps when you want to sway the peasants.

Is this what you believe about inspiration? **Yes___ No___**

    3. Partial Inspiration Theory - This is the belief that the **portions of Scripture concerning Divine revelation are inspired by God.** Those who espouse this theory reject anything the Bible says concerning science (creation), history (they say Moses was a "poetical" person, not a real one), or geography (Israel's right to Palestine). Brooke Foss Westcott, the Cambridge scholar who worked so hard to overthrow the authority of the Textus Receptus and replace it with his personal text, made no attempt to hide his belief that Moses and David existed only in Jewish poetry; he didn't believe either one really existed in history.

Is this what you believe about inspiration? **Yes___ No___**

    4. Concept Theory - This is the belief that the Bible contains God's **ideas** but not His exact **words.** In other words men used their own words to get across whatever God wanted to say.

    This is the theory followed by the translators of the Good News For Modern Man, New International Version and The Living Bible. It is disguised within the technical sounding title, "Dynamic Equivalence." This simply means that there were many times the translators **ignored** the words of the

Is Our English Bible Inspired?

Hebrew or Greek text they were using and simply wrote what they thought God was trying to say.

One of the greatest passages in Scripture which assures us that God would have His Divine hand involved in both the **inspiration** as well as the **preservation** of Scripture is found in Psalm 12. Ps. 12:6 The words of the LORD are pure words: as silver tried in a furnace of earth, purified seven times. Ps. 12:7 Thou shalt keep them, O LORD, thou shalt preserve them from this generation for ever.

The Hebrew of Psalm 12:7, Thou shalt keep **them**, O LORD, thou shalt preserve **them** from this generation for ever., is **third person plural** ("they" or "them") which makes the subject of the preservation being referred to in verse seven the "words" of verse six.

In spite of this, the translators of the New International Version felt they knew better than the writer and translated Psalm 12:7 in the **first** person plural ("we" or "us") to read, O Lord, you will keep **us** safe and protect **us** from such people forever. **THERE IS NO HEBREW AUTHORITY FOR THIS TRANSLATION!** The NIV translators are trying to fool the reader into thinking that the "preservation" of verse seven is not referring to the "words" of verse six but rather to the "weak" mentioned in verse five. Since the Hebrew doesn't support this teaching they simply "correct the Hebrew with their English" and **force** the Bible to say something it **never** said.[1]

---

1. If the reader fears that verse seven just might be referring to the "poor" of verse five rather than the "words" of verse six there is a simple way to find out. **Examine the entire psalm and see what the subject is!** The subject of this psalm is not "the weak." It is a comparison of the words of the wicked versus the words of the Lord. In

Sam Gipp

Is this what you believe about inspiration? **Yes___ No___**

5. Mechanical Dictation Theory - This is the belief that the men penning scripture were similar to a secretary taking a letter. God said the words He wanted written, the human vessels dutifully wrote those precise words down.

Is this what you believe about inspiration? **Yes___ No___**

6. Verbal Plenary Inspiration Theory - This is the belief that God chose **every word** used in the writing of the Bible. This includes writing, quoting the words of men, spontaneous statements and everything else that appears in Scripture.

Is this what you believe about inspiration? **Yes___ No___**

It Isn't That Easy

The **fact** is, "inspiration" cannot be as rigidly defined as Man would like. There are numerous areas in the Bible that simply defy being wedged into a "Yes" or "No" definition of Scripture.

1. John 4:37 And herein is that saying true, One soweth, and another reapeth. With what would seem a casual statement, Jesus assigns **inspiration** to a statement made long before He was on earth. A statement that is not even recorded in Scripture until He quotes it. Now, you need to answer one question, when was this statement "inspired?" Was it when it

---

verse two we find that the wicked "speak" with flattering "lips." Verse three is a condemnation of "flattering lips and the tongue that speaketh proud things:" In verse four the wicked "said" something with their "tongue" and "lips." The subject of the entire psalm is "words" not the "weak." The NIV translators violated Scripture by changing a clear passage so it would fit their prejudice against the preservation of the words of God.

was first made by someone we do not know? If so, did "Scripture" lie dormant until the Lord rescued it from oblivion and quoted it, assuring its rightful place in the Bible? Or was it simply the wise saying of some wizened prognosticator and received the "stamp" of inspiration when the Lord quoted it?

2. The Apostle Paul quoted **unsaved poets** in his **inspired** writings. He did this in Acts 17:28 and again in Titus 1:12.

3. In 1 Samuel 24:13 David quotes the words, "Wickedness proceedeth from the wicked:" which he ascribes to something known as "the proverb of the ancients."

Because these very words are recorded in Scripture, in the above mentioned quotations we assign (rightfully so) inspiration to them. Yet we are now faced with several very difficult questions: Were "Wickedness proceedeth from the wicked:" and "The Cretians are always liars, evil beasts, slow bellies" inspired by God **when originally stated** or when David and Paul quoted them? Could these words have remained for years "uninspired" and then receive some kind of "Divine anointing" because of the incidental (or God appointed) usage by a king or an Apostle? Could there be any other words like these laying around waiting to be "inspired" in such a manner?

The Plot Thickens!

While you ponder that, consider a couple other problem areas that defy an easily defined "blanket statement" on inspiration.

There are numerous times when God **apparently** inspired words from the mouth of someone who **didn't know** that what they were saying was inspired. This was the case in **every** conversation such as the words spoken by Pharaoh to Moses, or the words of any lost king of Syria, Assyria, Babylon etc. when recorded in the Bible. The plainest example of this are the words spoken by Caiaphas in John 11:48 - 51. Here Caiaphas prophecies of the death of Jesus Christ for Israel and all mankind **yet he didn't know it!**

Yet there is still a **better** example found in the writings of Paul. In 1 Corinthians 7:12 he says, "But to the rest speak I, not the Lord:..." making it plain that what he is then stating is coming from **him**, not the Lord. Yet we all accept (correctly) that even these words, which he considered "uninspired," were indeed "God breathed."

Yet there are even more puzzling scenarios in our quest for a simple definition of inspiration. What do you do with Scripture which is ascribed to someone **who plainly didn't write it?** Case in point: the text of Jeremiah chapters 45-51. In Jeremiah 36:1,2 we see God give Jeremiah the prophet the mandate to write these words. Yet in verse 4 we see that Jeremiah didn't write any of them. Baruch did. In fact Baruch testifies to this in verses 17 and 18. So these words were apparently spoken by God to Jeremiah and then Jeremiah told Baruch what to write. Which of the six convenient definitions of Scripture given above does that fit? None. But are the words of Jeremiah 45-51 inspired by God? You'd better believe it!

We also must not ignore the strange inspiration of some of Solomon's proverbs. In Proverbs 4:3, 4 Solomon tells us that the remaining text of this proverb are **actually the words of his father, David**, as he remembers them. David said them but Solomon wrote them down possibly years later.

Is Our English Bible Inspired?

But things gets even "stickier" when you look at Proverbs 31. Here, in verse 1, Solomon tells us that the following words are those of **his mother, Bathsheba.** Were they "inspired" when Bathsheba said them or when Solomon wrote them down?

Don't overlook Romans 16:22 in all of this either where we find that Tertius wrote the words ascribed to Paul in the Epistle to the Romans.

So how can all of these seemingly contradictory examples of what we call Scripture exist without fitting our carefully stated definition of just what "Scripture" is? The answer is simple. **If you think you're going to understand God, you're in big trouble.** There is simply **no way** to fit all of the above mentioned examples into any one of the theories mentioned above. **God is God!** If you are going to give yourself to the belief that He really inspired a Book, then at some point you're also going to have to simply **believe** that it is perfect, **even though you can't explain how or why.** (That's what **"faith"** is!) Keep in mind the great truth that "Without faith it is impossible to please God." If you believed the Bible because you **understood it** then you would be believing by **sight** not by **faith.**[2]

Without a doubt some men did write the words of God mechanically but, as you have seen, this cannot be ascribed to every word in our Bible. So how do you define inspiration? Pastor Rick Sowell said it best when he stated, "The

---

2. Apply this same faith concerning the question of **preservation.** If you could answer **all** of the questions that Bible critics come up with then you would believe the Bible is perfect by **sight** and not by **faith.** I am **very** comfortable with my **faith** in God.

inspiration of the scripture is the divine process by which God conveys His Words through man to man in such a miraculous manner that the personality of the human instrument is discernable, yet the Words are as truly the exact Words of God as if they had been written down by God Himself."

The final word on what words are inspired and what words are not is simple: if it's **in** the Bible **it's inspired**. (This simplistic "backwoods" definition will send shivers of terror down the spine of the man who worships at the altar of the great god, "Academia.")

Is this what you believe about inspiration? **Yes**___ **No**___

Is Our English Bible Inspired?

"It is impossible to rightly govern the world without God and the Bible."

George Washington

Is Our English Bible Inspired?

3
We Stand on Two Legs, Not One

You need to realize that the Bible sits upon **two** great pillars, not one. When many people think of the Bible, they envision it as standing on a pedestal. That pedestal being labeled, "Inspiration." But this is not accurate. The Bible actually rests on a platform held up by **two** pillars, **both** of which are necessary to its infallibility. **Both** are equal in importance and each is useless without the other. If one pillar is removed, the platform is off balance and the Bible will fall from its position of perceived infallibility.

It isn't that the Bible would not be inspired but that it would not be **perceived** to be inspired. What good is an inspired Book if no one **believes** it is inspired? No one will read it. If they do, they will not ascribe its words to God and thus will view it as any other man-written document.

The two pillars that undergird Scripture are **Inspiration** and

Preservation. If God did not inspire the Bible, then "preservation" is irrelevant since there is nothing to "preserve." If God did not preserve that which He inspired, then there is no perfect Bible on this earth anywhere right now. The claim of infallibility for the Bible was only relevant for the generation that held the original autographs in their hand. Every generation after that had either a mere copy or translation. Thus, no one today could **honestly** say that the Bible is infallible.

If God inspired the Bible without error in the Originals and then allowed it to be lost over the centuries, then it was senseless to inspire it in the first place. Inspiration without preservation is a "Divine waste of time."

The Two Pillars

Let's examine the two pillars and their importance in this issue.

Obviously, the claim of inspiration is what makes the Bible different from other books as well as divine. If it is not inspired of God, then it is just another work of men, wise men perhaps, but men; a "good" book, but just a "book," nonetheless.

THE CORRECT VIEW —

But if **God** was active in its creation then it is **not** a "good" book on a list of other "good" books. It is **the** Good

Book. Take a sheet of paper and number from 1-100. Put the Bible as number 1...**and leave the other 99 spaces blank!**

Think about this. Our world is a closed system. Even our scientists have to admit that. They also admit it is a degenerating system. Thus, **everything** in our world is **generated** from within a **dying system**. The very **best** book you can read (including this one) was generated from within and is a product of a dying system.

It is hopeless.

Therefore, you can see what a great and gracious act it was for God to insert something **divine** into our closed system. Something from **outside** the system. Something from His home, Heaven, to our home, Earth. The Bible is the **only Source** anyone can contact from **outside** this dying system. It is only through the Bible that mankind has access to the mind of God.

The First Pillar: Inspiration

Without a doubt, God inspired the Originals. There are several things we need to establish concerning the Originals:

1. Unlike other books, such as the Koran, the words in the Bible come from God, not man. They are divine. They are inspired.

2. Since God cannot make a mistake, the Originals were without error.

3. There was **never** a time in history when all of the Originals were in one binding. This is true even if we consider only the twenty-seven books of the New Testament. Think about it Paul wrote epistles, **letters,** to churches in several different locations. One went off to Rome, another to; Galatia, Philippi, Colosse, Ephesus while several went to Corinth, to name just a few.

First Corinthians was written around 57 AD. Second Corinthians was written a year later. Do you believe Paul kept his first letter around until he finished his second? Then did he keep these two around until 62 AD when he wrote his epistle to Ephesus and 63 AD when he wrote to Philippi? Do you understand that there was never a time when all twenty-seven original autographs were even in the same **room** let alone in one binding. The New Testament, as we know it, wasn't collated into one volume until Desiderius Erasmus (1466 - 1536) produced his first Greek New Testament in 1516.

4. The Originals are long gone. There are probably many reasons they have disappeared.

1. Many were destroyed when they became too worn to be read with any confidence in the text. Since they had been copied it was safe to destroy them. (The early Christian did not reverence the Originals as many seem to today.)

2. Some were probably destroyed by enemies of the Bible. During the rule of the Roman Emperor Diocletian, in the fourth century, there arose a great persecution against Christians. This led to the wanton destruction of all Christian writings. Antioch was his special target which brought about the senseless destruction of many priceless copies of Scripture. By the end of the first century, Antioch had more than 100,000 Christians among its

population. By the end of Diocletian's terror the number of Believers in Antioch had been greatly reduced.

    3. Some may have been destroyed by fire or natural disasters.

  Someone may infer that God didn't do a very good job of "preserving" His Bible if He allowed the Originals to disappear, but in a later chapter we will see the value God placed on the ink and papyrus of the original writings.

The Second Pillar: Preservation

  That the originals were inspired perfect in their entirety is an undisputed belief among Fundamentalists today. Many Fundamentalists, but not all, argue that only the Originals were perfect. They say that today you have nothing but copies and translations of those copies. They seem indignant at the thought that any "mere translation" should be considered a perfect copy of the originals. They claim that copies and translations are products of uninspired men and therefore must all contain mistakes.

  Clinging to this tenet is misleading. The folly in accepting this erroneous teaching is fourfold:

  1. It is somewhat confusing and unexplainable that a person could claim that God could not use sinful men **to preserve** His words, when all Fundamentalists believe that he used sinful men **to write** His inspired words. Look at the "pedigree" of several writers of Scripture.

    1. Moses and David, guilty of **murder**

2. David, guilty of **adultery**
3. Solomon, guilty of **idolatry**
4. Peter, guilty of **denying the Lord**

Certainly a God who had enough power to overcome human nature to inspire His words would also have enough power to overcome human nature to preserve them. Do you suppose that God has lost such ability over the years? I don't think so.

When some men talk about inspiration they wax bold and defiant that anyone would dare to question or doubt the inspiration of the Originals. Yet these same men shrink when confronted with the thought that the **same God** who inspired those autographs to be without error could possibly **preserve** them without error.

2. Those who believe in Divine inspiration **without** Divine preservation cannot explain why God would inspire the Originals and then lose them. Why give a perfect Bible to men like Peter, John, James, Andrew and company and not you? They had seen, heard, and touched the Lord (I John 1:1). You have not! If anyone ever needed a perfect Bible it is **you**, two thousand years removed from a Saviour you have never seen! Yet many modern-day Fundamentalists believe this very thing. Those who saw, heard and touched the Lord **also** had the added benefit of having the **only** perfect Bible that was ever on earth. The generations following had nothing.

Why would God go to all the trouble of **inspiring** a Book over a period of 1,500 years, using 40 different men, if He intended on **losing it** as soon as the job was complete? Could He not have **afforded** some errors in His originals, just as some believe He has allowed some errors in today's Bible, if He wasn't going to keep it around long anyway? Or do critics of God's perfect Bible believe that God was **unable** to prevent errors in the copies, even though He was able to prevent errors in the original autographs? It would seem like only **half** of a God who had the power to inspire but not preserve.

    3. As stated earlier, it is "Coward's Faith" which cannot be tested. In other words, it is rather safe to believe in a perfect set of originals which have been **lost**. Since they are lost, no one can ever practically challenge such a belief. Adherents to such a shallow persuasion can rest safely in the fact that they will never be proven wrong since the evidence needed to prove them wrong (the Originals) no longer exists.

    But if they dare put the same faith in a Bible **available today**, they know that they will definitely be bloodied defending their faith. King James Bible believers are called names, oppressed by unscrupulous brethren, lied about, ostracized and ridiculed for having the courage to have such faith. Thus, to believe in a perfect set of originals, but not to believe in a perfect English Bible, is **to believe nothing at all**.

    4. Regardless of their arguments against the doctrine of a preserved perfect Bible, such a fact is as much guaranteed by Scripture as the bodily return of Jesus Christ. If Psalm 12:7 is not to be taken literally then why take Acts 1:8 literally?

The Two Divine Pillars

    As stated earlier, the Bible stands on **two** pillars of truth, not one. It stands on the pillar of "Inspiration" and the equally important pillar of "Preservation."

1. In the case of Inspiration. If the Bible was not inspired then there was nothing to preserve. If God did not have His Divine hand in its creation then it is just another book written by men. Its value stands only in how well it can address the problems of today's world with the wisdom of an ancient world. In that respect it would indeed be "out of step with the times" if it wasn't inspired.

PRESERVATION WITHOUT INSPIRATION

If the Bible was not inspired of God, then there is no need of a divine act of preservation. After all, why should God expend any energy to preserve a book that He refused to expend any energy to create? If He did not inspire the Bible, then to preserve it would have been a greater effort on His part than He used in its generation.

Preservation without inspiration is impossible. If nothing was inspired then there is nothing that can be preserved. God's promise of Psalm 12:7 is useless.

2. In the case of Preservation. If God inspired the Bible and then was not active in preserving it across history, then His initial act of inspiration was **a waste of His time and effort**. If He did not intend to preserve His words when He inspired them, then He mistreated every generation of people in history since the Apostles, for only the original writers ever held an inspired

INSPIRATION WITHOUT PRESERVATION

Is Our English Bible Inspired?

autograph in their hand. But at that, they only held the autograph that **they** had written. They may never have held the work of another inspired writer. For even the Apostles did not possess the original autographs of Moses or the early Old Testament writers or of other New Testament writers.

If there is no preservation, then the words of God which were on this earth at one time are now **lost**. They never made the journey across history. The God who inspired them lacked either the ability or resolve to preserve them.

As stated earlier, **inspiration without preservation was a Divine waste of time.** If there is no first pillar there is no need for the second. If there is no second pillar then the purpose of the first was defeated by the actions of feeble men; the **same kind of men** that God was able to use to write His words perfectly in the first place. Either pillar standing alone is worthless. Inspiration without preservation means only a handful of people in history ever saw, at best, a small portion of the Bible. Furthermore, the case for preservation does not exist if there was no inspiration in the first place.

Therefore, the doctrine of **Divine Inspiration** is useless without the doctrine of **Divine Preservation**. The Bible does not stand on one pillar, but two. To preserve what was never inspired is impossible. To inspire and not preserve is foolish.

Furthermore, why would a God Who overcame men's humanity to **write** His words turn the preservation of them over to those same fallible men? No scholar, no holy man, no scientist could possibly preserve God's divine words. Why would God excuse Himself from duty when it comes to preserving that which He initiated? If preservation were left up to fallible men, then it would be as impossible to have a perfect Bible as it would be if He left the original writing up to fallible men. But, if God used the **same** divine power to see to it that His words were preserved across history as He did in inspiring them, then you can have a perfect copy of those words today.

It's called, the **King James Bible.**

THE CORRECT VIEW —

Is Our English Bible Inspired?

"...knowledge of the Bible without a college course is more valuable than a college course without the Bible."

William Lyon Phelps

4
How Important Are the Originals?

Many say we should be loyal to the Originals and not to a mere translation. This sounds both noble and dogmatic. It is neither. The truth is we should put as much value on the Originals as God does. Since the Originals no longer exist, any sincere student of Scripture must realize that either God didn't regard the Originals highly enough to bother preserving them, or He wanted to but failed. We **know** the latter isn't true. Let's examine the former.

More Emphasis Then God

It's easy to beat one's chest and "boldly" proclaim loyalty to the Originals, which no longer exist. But there must be a standard that can be tested. One thing we do not want to do is put more emphasis on something than God does. If you put more emphasis on the Originals than God does you will end up with an idol. Take what has happened to Mary, the mother of Jesus, within the Roman Catholic Church:

1. Mary was the mother of Jesus - **True**
2. Mary was the mother of **God**. - **False**
3. Mary was a virgin when Jesus was born. - **True**

4. Mary was a "perpetual" virgin. - **False**

We know that two of the four statements above are true and two are **beyond reality**. We accept the two true ones. Thus, we respect Mary as the Lord's mother but assign no special value to her.

The Roman Catholic Church, on the other hand, believes the answer to all four statements is "True." What is the result? Idolatry. Why? Because when you **make more of something than GOD does you end up with an idol!** We don't want to put more emphasis on the Originals lest we end up like the Catholics.

Original #1

In Jeremiah chapter 36 we are told that the prophet Jeremiah had written a roll of a book at the urging of the Holy Spirit.

1 And it came to pass in the fourth year of Jehoiakim the son of Josiah king of Judah, that this word came unto Jeremiah from the LORD, saying,
2 Take thee a roll of a book, and write therein all the words that I have spoken unto thee against Israel, and against Judah, and against all the nations, from the day I spake unto thee, from the days of Josiah, even unto this day.

In verse 21 this roll is brought before King Jehoiakim and read by his servant Jehudi. According to verse 23 Jehudi read three or four leaves and then King Jehoiakim got so upset that he cut it up with a penknife and cast it into the fire on the hearth until it was destroyed.

Is Our English Bible Inspired?

21 So the king sent Jehudi to fetch the roll: and he took it out of Elishama the scribe's chamber. And Jehudi read it in the ears of the king, and in the ears of all the princes which stood beside the king. **22** Now the king sat in the winterhouse in the ninth month: and there was a fire on the hearth burning before him. **23** And it came to pass, that when Jehudi had read three or four leaves, he cut it with the penknife, and cast it into the fire that was on the hearth, until all the roll was consumed in the fire that was on the hearth.

Thus ends the ORIGINAL!

Original #2

Then the Lord moved Jeremiah to rewrite the roll adding some words to it. (Jeremiah 36:32)

28 Take thee again another roll, and write in it all the former words that were in the first roll, which Jehoiakim the king of Judah hath burned.
32 Then took Jeremiah another roll, and gave it to Baruch the scribe, the son of Neriah; who wrote therein from the mouth of Jeremiah all the words of the book which Jehoiakim king of Judah had burned in the fire: and there were **added besides unto them many like words**. (Think these words were in italics?)

Thus ORIGINAL #2 is born. It should be no surprise to those who **really** believe in the omnipotence of God that He could reproduce His writings after they had been destroyed. Do you suppose God is "guilty" of "Double Inspiration?" Would **you** like to bring the charge against Him?

If you want to know what this twice inspired manuscript said simply turn to Jeremiah 45 and don't stop reading until you finish chapter fifty-one. All you need to do to verify this is read Jeremiah 45:1, which says,

1 The word that Jeremiah the prophet spake unto Baruch the son of Neriah, when he had written these words in a book at the mouth of Jeremiah, in the fourth year of Jehoiakim the son of Josiah king of Judah, saying,

This is the same thing Jeremiah 36:1 says. Jeremiah told Seraiah to read this roll, what we know as Jer. 45-51, when he came into Babylon (Jeremiah 51:59-61). After Seraiah finished reading the roll Jeremiah instructed him to bind a stone to it and **cast it into the Euphrates river.** (Jeremiah 51:63)
Thus ends ORIGINAL #2!
Here we have one original destroyed by a wicked king. That may be understandable. Then God "re-inspires" the destroyed manuscript and then has it **destroyed** after its message has been delivered.

Original #3

But that's not the most amazing thing that takes place in this transaction. We all have a copy of the text of this roll in chapters 45-51 of Jeremiah. Where did it come from? It couldn't have come from ORIGINAL #1 because that was destroyed by King Jehoiakim. It couldn't have come from ORIGINAL #2, that was destroyed when Seraiah threw it into the Euphrates river. It obviously came from a **copy** of ORIGINAL #2 which we can only call ORIGINAL #3!
This creates two very big problems for those who overemphasize the "Originals."
1 Every Bible ever printed with a copy of Jeremiah in it has the text in chapters 45-51 which is translated from a copy of the second "original," or ORIGINAL #3.

Is Our English Bible Inspired?

2 Secondly, **no one** can overlook the fact that God didn't have the least bit of interest in preserving the "original" **once it had been copied and its message delivered.** So **why** should we put more emphasis on the Originals than God does? An emphasis which is plainly unscriptural. It is evident from what takes place in the book of Jeremiah that, once the message has been delivered, God is not the least bit interested in preserving the Originals. In fact, He may have destroyed them so that future scholars couldn't make an idol out of them!

Since we have the text of the Originals preserved in the King James Bible, we have no need of the Originals themselves.

"The Bible is the source of liberty."
                                    Thomas Jefferson

5
Can a Translation Be Inspired?

Many a Bible college student has heard a "fearless" professor declare, "The King James Bible is just a translation and **everybody** knows that a translation can't be inspired." The answer to this bold-sounding statement is simple. The **Bible**, not a self-important college professor, is our **final authority** in **all matters** of faith and practice. Where is there a **Scripture** that says a translation can't be inspired?

Before you throw this book down and write me off, let's consult our "final authority in all matters of faith and practice" to see how it deals with the subject of inspired translations.

There are **at least** three times within Scripture that we can find an "inspired translation."

I. The First Inspired Translation
   A. Genesis 42 - 45
      1. In the Book of Genesis, chapters 42-45, is the record of Joseph's reunion with his brethren. That Joseph spoke Egyptian instead of Hebrew is evident by Genesis 42:23.

23 "And they knew not that Joseph understood them; for he spake unto them by **an interpreter**."

2. The participants
    a. Joseph **spoke** Egyptian
    b. the Egyptian interpreter **spoke** Hebrew
    c. Moses **wrote** in Hebrew when he wrote it down

    It is, of course, an accepted fact that no translation can be "word perfect." Therefore, you know that the Hebrew translation of Joseph's Egyptian statements as found in the Old Testament manuscripts **cannot** be an exact word for word reproduction. You are left with quite a dilemma. **Whom** did God inspire? Did He inspire the statements Joseph made in Egyptian, the Egyptian interpreter's verbal translation, or Moses' written translation as found in the Hebrew of the Old Testament? (Is thinking painful for you?)

    First we must concede a **fact** of history and that is there is no copy of Genesis found **anywhere** that contains Joseph's words written in Egyptian. If God inspired Joseph, was his "original" statement marred by his Egyptian interpreter, or by Moses' translation? Or did God inspire Moses to pen an "inspired translation" which would fly in the face of many Fundamentalists' claim that a translation cannot be inspired?

    Whether you ascribe inspiration to Joseph's Egyptian interpreter's **statements** or not, (and you **should**) you **must** grant that what Moses **wrote** in Hebrew truly was inspired. Thus, this represents an "inspired translation."

II. The Second Inspired Translation
A. Acts 22:1- 21

1. After Paul's arrest in Acts 21 he was given permission to plead his case with the Jews. Acts 21:40 informs us that he spoke to them in Hebrew.

40 "And when he had given him licence, Paul stood on the stairs, and beckoned with the hand unto the people. And when there was made a great silence, he spake unto them **in the Hebrew tongue**, saying,"

2. Every word in Acts 22:1 - 21 was **spoken** in Hebrew.

3. Luke **wrote** it all out in Greek.

4. There is **not one** manuscript extant, anywhere, of Acts 22 which records Paul's statement in Hebrew.

What was inspired? The words Paul spoke in Hebrew or the words Luke wrote in Greek?

Again whether or not you ascribe inspiration to Paul's Hebrew **statement** or not, (and you **should**) you **must** grant that what Luke **wrote** in Greek was inspired. Thus, this represents another "inspired translation."

At this point I have had a less than honest opponent of the King James Bible "crawdad" and claim, "Since neither Joseph nor Paul's statements were written down at the time, then the inspiration occurred when Moses and Luke wrote, therefore these are not **really** examples of inspired translations."

Now, an **honest** person would have to admit that **both** written accounts are indeed translations of the earlier statements and **are** inspired. Therefore they **would have to** qualify as "inspired translations." But, there is an **indisputable way** of derailing the train of a dishonest doubter. The answer is childishly simple and revolves around the bedrock definition of "inspiration." Many like to visit "the Greek" and solemnly declare that "inspiration" means "God breathed." They then pontificate that the words were "breathed" by God. Fine, then we all admit that if **God** spoke, it **would have to be inspired**. Let's see how that lines up with our third example of an "inspired translation."

III. The Third Inspired Translation
A. Acts 9:5, 6 cf. Acts 26:14

Acts 9:5, 6 records the words that the Lord Jesus Christ said to Saul during their encounter on the road to Damascus. While giving his testimony before Agrippa, Paul says in Acts 26:14:

> 14 "And when we were all fallen to the earth, I heard a voice speaking unto me, and saying **in the Hebrew tongue**, Saul, Saul, why persecutest thou me? it is hard for thee to kick against the pricks."

    1. Jesus **spoke** Hebrew.
    2. Luke **wrote** it all out in Greek.
    3. There is **no** manuscript extant of Acts 9 which records Jesus' statement in Hebrew.

What was inspired? Would anyone dare try to say that the words Jesus spoke in Hebrew were not "God breathed?" Would anyone dare try to say that the words Luke wrote in Greek were not inspired? It is painfully obvious to the doubter that both **what Jesus spoke** and **what Luke wrote** were **both** inspired! Therefore there is no denying that the original statement **as well as** the translation **were inspired**.

Thankfully no college professor, scholar, pastor or any other fallible human being is our "final authority in all matters of faith and practice." Therefore, where a man and the Bible don't line up, even if a man is our good friend, **the man** is wrong **every time**.

Are you saying "Amen" right now or trying to make excuse for your lack of faith?

"So great is my veneration of the Bible that the earlier my children begin to read it, the more confident will be my hope that they will prove useful citizens to their country and respectable members of society. I have for many years made it a practice to read through the Bible once a year."

John Quincy Adams

6
Translations vs the Originals

We have all heard someone make the bold declaration that a translation can't be as good as the Original. What do you think? Before you even **think** about answering you should know by now that what you think **doesn't matter** if it is contrary to what the Bible says on **any** subject. The fact is that God gave us His word just so we **wouldn't** be slaves to the opinions of men. So, let's go and see what our **final authority** in **all matters** of faith and practice has to say on the subject. Most of the time with issues like this, it isn't that the Bible is silent on the subject, but rather that men **think** it doesn't say anything about it, so they turn to human reason and exalt it above the Bible. If the human reasoning comes from a "scholar," then it seems to carry an almost sacred authority with it. If we accept as fact statements of men that are not supported by the Scripture, then we need to throw our Bible away right now and worship our favorite scholar-guru, for then, the Bible is not our final authority in all matters of faith and practice. We believe in sacred authority, but we ascribe it to the Bible rather than a walking, talking dirt ball.

Checking the Authority

Don't you think that the simplest way to study about "originals" and "translations" would be to simply go to our "final authority" and look up the word "translate" to see how a translation compares to an original **in Scripture**?

The first thing we need to do is to establish what the final results of our research can be. In this case you **must** come to one of **three** conclusions.

1. A translation is INFERIOR to the Originals

This is basically the stand a **faithless** man takes. It is always accepted, based on a statement made by some well educated professor, with no factual backing whatsoever. It is just an opinion. But regardless, you must be willing to accept that it is true **if the Bible proves it**.

2. A translation is EQUAL to the Originals

This is just as much an option as the first. If, **through careful study of the Bible** concerning the subject of translations, it seems that both are equal then you will have to abandon whatever previous position you had for the scriptural one.

3. A translation is SUPERIOR to the Originals

The thought of this being true is so unpleasant for many preachers and teachers that they cannot even be honest enough to review the biblical evidence lest their prejudice not survive the light of Scripture.

If you check your Bible, (I didn't say "your computer") you will find that the word "translate" only appears **five times** in Scripture in **three different places**.

There are three translations spoken of in the Bible. Since we accept the Bible as our **final** authority in all matters of faith and practice, its "practice" concerning translations

Is Our English Bible Inspired?

will have more authority than any mere human opinion, yours, mine or anyone elses.

Let's examine the three translations referred to in Scripture.

I. The First Translation
A. 2 Samuel 3:7-10

The first translation mentioned in Scripture is found in 2 Samuel 3:7-10:

> **7** And Saul had a concubine, whose name was Rizpah, the daughter of Aiah: and Ish-bosheth said to Abner, Wherefore hast thou gone in unto my father's concubine?
> **8** Then was Abner very wroth for the words of Ish-bosheth, and said, Am I a dog's head, which against Judah do shew kindness this day unto the house of Saul thy father, to his brethren, and to his friends, and have not delivered thee into the hand of David, that thou chargest me to day with a fault concerning this woman?
> **9** So do God to Abner, and more also, except, as the LORD hath sworn to David, even so I do to him;
> **10** To **translate the kingdom** from the house of Saul, and to set up the throne of David over Israel and over Judah, from Dan even to Beersheba.

After the death of King Saul, in 1 Samuel 31, Abner, the captain of Saul's army, installed Ish-bosheth as King instead of David (2 Samuel 12:8,9).

Later Ish-bosheth and Abner had a falling out. Abner, in anger, announced to Ish-bosheth that he was going to "translate" the Kingdom of Israel from Ish-bosheth to David.

It is obvious by Abner's statement of 2 Samuel 3:9 that the LORD wanted David to be king over all twelve tribes of Israel. This is not to be confused with the 10-2 split that

God instituted in 1 Kings 11:29-32. This split kingdom was the product of the greed and self-service of both Ish-bosheth and Abner and **was not** the desire of God.

   B. **The conditions of this "translation"**
   1. **The "Original"**
      a. The kingdom is divided contrary to God's will. David has a portion and Ish-bosheth has a portion. Yet 2 Samuel 3:9 reveals the Lord **wanted** David to have the **entire** kingdom.
   2. **The "Translation"**
      a. David ends up being king over the entire kingdom. This is what the Lord wanted in the first place.
   3. **The End Product**
      a. The translation is **superior** to the original.

The first thing we see is that the result of this translation is **not equal** with the original condition. Furthermore, no **honest person** can pretend to believe the result is **inferior** as compared to the original. Therefore, in this case at least, the translation is clearly **superior** to the original.

II. The Second Translation
   A. **Colossians 1:13**

   13 Who hath delivered us from the power of darkness, and **hath translated us** into the kingdom of his dear Son:

This translation obviously has to do with our salvation. At one time you were under the power of darkness but when you trusted Jesus Christ as your personal Saviour

you were "translated" into the kingdom of God. **Definitely** an improvement.
> **B. The conditions of this "translation"**
> **1. The "Original"**
>> **a.** You were **lost** and under the *"power of darkness."*
>
> **2. The "Translation"**
>> **a.** You were **saved** and no longer under the *"power of darkness."*
>
> **3. The End Product**
>> **a.** The translation is **superior** to the original.

Once again the translation is neither equal nor inferior to the original. Would you say that being saved is worse or equal to being lost?

III. The Third Translation
> **A. Hebrews 11:5**
>> 5 By faith **Enoch was translated** that he should not see death; and was not found, because **God had translated him**: for before **his translation** he had this testimony, that he pleased God.

Enoch's translation was a type of the Blessed Hope spoken of in Titus 2:13. That is when believers will be translated from this world to Heaven. Again, an obvious improvement over the "original."
> **B. The conditions of this "translation"**
> **1. The "Original"**
>> **a.** Enoch was a godly man who was living in a world whose imagination was *"only evil continually."*
>>
>> **b.** Someday he would die in that world.

2. The "Translation"
   a. Enoch is **translated** alive to Heaven so that he would not see death.
   b. This act is a type of the rapture of the Church.
3. The End Product
   a. The translation is **superior** to the original.

We see then that, in our **final authority** in **all matters** of faith and practice a translation is never equal or inferior to an original. It is **always** superior. If you dislike this truth you may wish to hold your breath or throw yourself on the floor and kick your feet, but it will not change the truth! If you are a simple Bible believer you will have no trouble accepting this. If you worship education or just hate to be wrong, you will reject this Bible **fact** as easily as you have rejected every other Bible fact that you couldn't agree with because it tested your faith. What will you do?

A Three-point Sermon

These three passages dovetail into a perfect sermon, for they represent three different translations that every human needs.

Three Translations You Need
1. Salvation - Col. 1:13
   A. You need to trust Jesus Christ as your personal Saviour. Without trusting Christ the soul is damned to a Lake of Fire. Jesus Christ died, paid for the sins of all mankind and rose again the third day to save all men from this fate.

2. **2 Samuel 3:10**
    A. You then need to "translate" your kingdom to Heaven where *"moth and rust doth not corrupt and thieves do not break through and steal."*
3. **Hebrews 11:5**
    A. Someday the Lord will return to take believers to Heaven. Christians have been awaiting this event since the first century. If this happens in your lifetime, you, like Enoch, will go straight to Heaven without having to die.

The Advantages of Any Translation over the Originals

If translations are **really** superior to the Original then the King James Bible, a translation, should be superior to the Original in some **obvious** way. In fact, there are five areas where **any** translation is superior, **NOT MORE INSPIRED**, but **superior**, to the Originals.

1. The whole Bible in one volume

As already mentioned, there has **never** been a time in history when all sixty-six **original manuscripts** of the books of the Bible were ever bound into one volume. Moses' copy of Genesis **was never** bound in the same book with the Apostle John's copy of Revelation. There was **never** a time when anyone could hold all sixty-six original autographs in one hand. Yet you can hold **every book of the Bible** in one hand through the improvement of having a translation. It's not "more inspired," it's just an improvement over the Original.

The translation is superior to the Original.

2. Chapter & verse divisions

Recall how many times you have heard a preacher or teacher say, "Turn to this book, chapter and verse..." This could not be done with the Originals. They were written on scrolls or large vellum codice that had no chapter and verse divisions. Bible study of any sort, as we know it, could not be carried on with any of the original manuscripts. Imagine trying to conveniently turn to a portion of Scripture in the **middle** of Isaiah, then at the **end**, then back to the about the fifth chapter. This is impossible without chapter and verse markings.

The translation is superior to the Original.

3. More durable

Even an inexpensive Bible is far more durable than the materials used for the Originals. Today's Bibles have expensive bindings, special inks, India paper. The fragile papyrus of Originals would never last as long as the Bibles we possess today.

The translation is superior to the Original.

4. The language is superior

It can be said that **more people speak English than ever** spoke Hebrew or Greek. Chinese soldiers speak English. Japanese businessmen speak English. Russian airline pilots speak English. It has covered far more of the globe than Hebrew and Greek ever did combined. More people today have access to the Scripture through use of English than through Hebrew or Greek.

The translation is superior to the Original.

5. Multiple copies

As stated above, the sixty-six original autographs were **never** bound into a single volume. But, even

Is Our English Bible Inspired?

if they had been, it would mean there had only ever been **one** Bible. **There could not be two.** If we were bound to the Originals, then only **one person** could have the Bible! Yet, today, most Christians have several Bibles. Not different versions but different styles. Today you can get a King James Bible in a multitude of sizes and styles. You can get a standard Bible, a large print edition, a wide margin edition, numerous "study" Bibles or just a particular color of leather cover, or you may simply want a New Testament. There are **millions** of copies of the Bible in circulation. This condition could **never** be true if all we had was the Originals.

The translation is superior to the Original.

Please understand, the translation is **not** "more inspired" than the Originals. It is simply an improvement over them. Just like the translations were in the biblical examples we examined.

The Modern Translators' Dilemma

Before we close this chapter I want you to think about something. Imagine being one of the translators of a modern Bible translation who **does not believe** that a translation **can even be as good** as an original, let alone superior. With this erroneous belief in tow, you arrive at each of the three passages of Scripture in which it was illustrated that the translation was an improvement over the original. What do you do when the Bible plainly teaches the opposite of your personal prejudice?

1. 2 Samuel 3:9, 10

If you are one of the translators of the New King James Version you would translate 2 Samuel 3:9, 10 as follows:

> **9** May God do so to Abner, and more also, if I do not do for David as the Lord has sworn to him—
> **10 to transfer** the kingdom from the house of Saul, and set up the throne of David over Israel and over Judah, from Dan to Beersheba.

It can be argued that "transfer" is exactly what Abner did to the kingdom. ("Translate" is just as accurate.) But you wouldn't want to **preach** "transfer" rather than "translate." We all know that we will receive rewards in Heaven for what we do down here. If we give money down here, we will receive some **equivalent** value when we get to Heaven. Now tell me, when you get to Heaven would you rather receive God's **equivalent** to what you gave or the **dollars themselves**? Just what would we do with "dollars" in a place where **the street** is made of gold?

2. Colossians 1:13

If you are one of the translators of the New American Standard Version you would translate Colossians 1:13 as follows:

> **13** For He rescued us from the domain of darkness, and **transferred us** to the kingdom of His beloved Son,

No one can dispute that there is a grand difference between "transferred" and "translated." What pastor hasn't

Is Our English Bible Inspired?

had someone "transfer" their membership from a very good church but later found out that the person wasn't even saved. (By the way, if someone tells you there are no inspired translations tell them **you are one!**)

3. Hebrews 11:5

> **5** By faith Enoch **was taken** from this life, so that he did not experience death; he could not be found, because **God had taken him away.** For before **he was taken**, he was commended as one who pleased God.

Here is another place where you definitely want to be "translated" rather than "taken." The Bible says we will be changed in a moment." Believe me, you want that. Have you ever imagined what you would do to the ceiling in your house at the Rapture if all the Lord did was tried to "take" you rather than "translate" you into a body likened unto His glorious body? (Phil. 3:21) In fact, that is the exact **reason** God is going to **translate** us before we go up. The bodies we have now couldn't pass through the hull of a submerged submarine, (**someone's** body is going to have to) but a glorified body will. (For you throw-backs from the '60s, I never read the NIV rendering of Hebrews 11:5 without singing..."They're coming to take me away! Ho ho! They're coming to take me away! He he! Ha ha, to the Funny Farm....) Hmm. The "Funny Farm?" Seems like that's where some of these modern translations come from!

"The Bible is a book in comparison with which all other in my eyes are of minor importance."

Gen. Robert E. Lee

7
The "T R Man"

It has been said that there are several hundred bibles. You can go to the average "Christian" bookstore and see as many as a dozen different English translations on the shelves. But this is deceiving, for there aren't thousands or hundreds or even three different bibles. There are only **two**. There are over 5,700 Greek manuscripts or manuscript fragments of the New Testament extant today. They can be classified in one of four ways.

1. Unclassified manuscripts - Many fragments are so tiny that they are too small to classify. These are known as "Unclassified manuscripts." There are about one hundred eighty manuscripts in this group.

2. "D" - This group of manuscripts consists of only eight manuscripts, even fewer than the Unclassified manuscripts. They have no input in the issue of Bible translations.

3. Alexandrian Family - This small group, less than sixty, originates from Alexandria, Egypt, and has been corrupted by the Egyptian influence. This is the basis for what is known as the "Critical text" which is the text used to produce most all modern translations.

4. Antiochan Family - This group originates from the center of New Testament Christianity, Antioch, Syria, and consist of over 5,400 manuscripts, many are complete copies of the entire New Testament. This is the source of the English translations prior to the King James Bible, the King James Bible itself and a few since then.

Every Bible on every Christian bookstore shelf is from either the Antiochan Family or the Alexandrian Family. Thus, there are only **two** Bibles.

But there is another heritage these two locations have left us. That is their view of the authority of the Bible.[3]

Christians in Antioch believed the Bible should be taken **literally**. They believed it was the inspired word of God and mistrusted philosophy and science. This **Antiochan Mentality** can be defined with one sentence: "The Bible is **perfect** and **cannot** be improved."

In Alexandria they did not believe the Bible to be of Divine origin and exalted both science and philosophy. This **Alexandrian Mentality** can be defined with one sentence: "The Bible is **not** perfect and **can** be improved."

Since there are two products of each location, there can be **four** different combinations.

---

3. For a more in depth study of the impact of the Antiochan and Alexandrian families, see this author's work entitled *An Understandable History of the Bible*, available through DayStar Publishing, www.daystarpublishing.com.

1. The Bible Corrector:
   a. Mentality - Alexandrian
   b. Manuscript Family - Alexandrian

This is someone who adheres to the **Alexandrian Mentality**: "The Bible is **not** perfect and **can** be improved." He also accepts the Alexandrian Family as the best source of truth. You will find him using anything from a New International Version to a Good News For Modern Man. He will be critical of the concept of a word-perfect Bible and sometimes even be antagonistic to Bible believers.

2. The Ignorant Christian:
   a. Mentality - Antiochan
   b. Manuscript Family - Alexandrian

This is someone who adheres to the **Antiochan Mentality**: "The Bible is **perfect** and **cannot** be improved," but accepts the **Alexandrian manuscripts**. They truly believe the Bible to be inerrant but have no idea of the "Two Bible" controversy. Some would say, "They're hypocrites!" No, not at all. They are **babies**. This is usually the situation you find new born, baby Christians in. Endued with childlike faith they believe with all their heart that the Bible is the perfect word of God. But, they may have gotten saved in a church that uses an NIV or NASV. They have no idea these are corrupt. They're not dishonest. They're babies.

3. The "TR Man":
   a. Mentality - Alexandrian
   b. Manuscript Family - Antiochan

Now this is the guy who can really mess up a young or unsuspecting Christian. They have the right Bible, the King

James. They will even beat their chest and boldly proclaim how they would never use "one of them modern perversions!" For all intents and purposes they look and sound like a "King James Man." But they are not. This man, in spite of using only a King James Bible, does **not** believe it is without error. They believe the King James is the best translation available from the Textus Receptus Greek text. Amazingly, they may be aware of their Alexandrian Mentality or they may be unaware they have it. What I mean is, when they say they believe the King James Bible is the perfect word of God they are **not** lying. They actually think they believe it. But they still believe all the standard Alexandrian teachings, such as:

    1. The italics don't belong in the Bible
    2. The "thees" and the "thous" stifle spiritual growth
    3. King James was a homosexual
    4. There are too many archaic words in the King James Bible
    5. Etc.

The **honest** ones love the Bible and are usually teachable. They do not realize that, while they are being loyal to the word of God with their **heart**, they are being disloyal to it with their mind. It is like a man **telling** everyone how much he loves his wife but he secretly thinks she's stupid and thinks his secretary is smarter. He is loyal to one with his heart and loyal to the other with his mind.

    This man is not to be blamed for his unconscious loyalty to Alexandria. He probably started out as an "Ignorant Christian" mentioned above and went to a Bible college that instilled the Alexandrian Mentality into his mind over a slow, three-year process. He trusted his college and, although it may have equipped him well in other areas, it failed him in this crucial one. Someday he will have to decide if he's going to be loyal to his Bible or his "Alma Mater."

The **dishonest** ones are dangerous. They usually have their heart set on some personal goal and they need to **look** like they believe the King James Bible to attain that goal. When backed into a corner they try to **redefine** what a "Bible believer" is. When they're done, their definition of a "Bible believer" describes someone who doesn't believe in a perfect Bible they can **hold in their hand**. But, strangely, their definition of a Bible believer looks an awful lot...**like them**.

4. The Bible believer:
    a. Mentality - Antiochan
    b. Manuscript Family - Antiochan

This is the gentleman who truly believes the Bible is perfect, without error. He believes the Originals were perfect and he believes the Bible that **he holds in his hand**, the King James Bible, is perfect.

Examine the four classes above and answer this question: which one places more faith in God than the other three?

The Illusion of Safety

Many preachers **want** to believe the Bible is perfect but they have heard the jokes told about Bible believers. They have heard them called "cultist." They have heard them belittled. They have heard education deified and Bible believers portrayed as backwoods hicks. But, most sadly, they have been convinced by a teacher they trusted that no Bible is without error.

Sam Gipp

Torn between the ridicule of truly believing their Bible is perfect and the benefits of **saying** they believe it, they think there is safety in retreating to the Greek text the King James Bible was translated from, the Textus Receptus. Even though they may dabble in the old, "the Greek says this" game, the fact is, they don't know Greek and know even less about the Greek text. But, few others know any more than they do so they feel protected by a shield of ignorance. Thus, they can now say they believe the "Bible (the Textus Receptus) is the perfect word of God."

Unfortunately their perceived safety can be shattered by just **one visit** to the text they claim is the "perfect word of God."

In 1 John 2:23 the King James Bible reads, Whosoever denieth the Son, the same hath not the Father: *[but] he that acknowledgeth the Son hath the Father also.*

You notice that the last half of the verse is in italics. That means those words had no Greek support. In fact, they were inserted from the Latin. The King James translators put them in the text but placed them in italics to show they believed they belonged in the text but had no Greek testimony for them.

You can see the dilemma a "TR Man" is faced with. A true Bible believer would say, "It's OK. They're in my Bible so they belong there." But someone who unknowingly "hung his hat" on the Textus Receptus is faced with the very Bible he **pretends** to believe, the King James, reading differently than the one he **really** believes, the Textus Receptus. By ignorantly elevating the Textus Receptus above the King James Bible, he has painted himself into a corner.

Fortunately there is a way out. **There is** Greek testimony for the last half of the verse. It was found in a

Is Our English Bible Inspired?

manuscript discovered about two hundred years after the seemingly prophetic King James translators placed those words in the English text. It was then verified by another Greek manuscript which was known to exist in the fifteenth century but was restricted from public view. Do you feel better now? Well you shouldn't! The two manuscripts just mentioned are Sinaiticus, discovered in 1841, and Vaticanus, known to exist since 1481 but withheld from examination by the owner, the Roman Catholic Church! These two **corrupt** manuscripts form the backbone of the **corrupt** Alexandrian family.

Now what does the TR man do? He doesn't want to say the portion doesn't belong in the Bible or he is admitting that his trusty "TR" has failed him. What should he do?

While you ponder that let me tell you what I believe. I believe the Textus Receptus is the best Greek text and is superior to the Critical Text which is based on the Alexandrian family of Greek manuscripts (which is the text used for most modern translations)... **but it's WRONG in 1 John2:23!** Furthermore I believe the Critical Text is error-riddled and the manuscripts it is based on, **especially** Sinaiticus and Vaticanus are corrupt...**but it's RIGHT in 1 John2:23!**

How do I know? Because I am a **King James Bible believer,** not a Textus Receptus believer or an Alexandrian believer. Why? Because I believe the King James Bible is the inspired, preserved word and words of God. **Not** the Textus Receptus. **Not** the Alexandrian family. It is the **book I hold in my hand!**

It is safer to accept the scorn and ridicule of faithless Bible correctors and **trust** that God gave us a perfect Bible than to cave in and seek a pat on the head from scholarship and insinuate that God **wanted** to fulfill Psalm 12:7 but just wasn't able to. I'll stick with **God!**

Is Our English Bible Inspired?

"The Bible is the best book in the world."

John Adams

Is Our English Bible Inspired?

8
Can You Correct the Greek With the English?

This question has the wrong wording. What is meant when someone asks that question is, "Can you correct the **Originals** with the English?" There is only one man I know of who believes he can correct the Originals with the English. His name is Dr. Ken Barker and he was the Executive Editor for the translation of the New International Version. In 1995 I debated the translators of several of the modern versions on the John Ankerberg television show. Dr. Barker was one of those present. During our debate we discussed God's promise of **preservation** as found in Psalm 12:7. This verse has been referred to in Chapter 2 of this book, Theories of Inspiration, but we will examine it more carefully at this time.

    7 *Thou shalt keep* **them***, O L*ORD*, thou shalt preserve* **them** *from this generation for ever.*

The translators of the New International Version have rendered this to read,

    7 *O L*ORD*, you will keep* **us** *safe and protect* **us** *from such people forever."*

As you can see where the Authorized Version reads "them" the NIV reads "us." This may seem like a minor point but it is far from minor. The Hebrew word translated "them" in the AV and "us" in the NIV is the word, "shamar," meaning "to keep." It is in the **future second person singular tense**, "thou shalt keep" and is directed to the **THIRD person plural** "they, them" and **not** the **first** person plural "we, us" as the New International Version translators rendered it. There is **no Hebrew manuscript anywhere in the world** that has "shamar" in the **first** person plural. That means there is **no Hebrew authority anywhere** for the erroneous translation found in the New International Version.

I challenged Dr. Barker on this on national television. His excuse for the erroneous, unsupported, NIV rendering was that **he believed** that verse seven was God's promise to preserve "the poor" mentioned in verse five, not "the words of the Lord" mentioned in verse six. Mind you, he said **he believed that**. He didn't (couldn't) say there was any Hebrew manuscript evidence for the NIV rendering. Thus, based on **nothing stronger than the opinion of a fallible man**, Dr. Barker **"corrected" the Original Hebrew with HIS English!** If Fundamentalists think it is heresy to claim to be able to correct the Original with the English, then they should loudly and vehemently condemn the practice as found in the New International Version.

The Seeds of Doubt

Unfortunately, once the seeds of doubt have been planted they seems always to remain dormant in the back of the mind: i.e. "What if Psalm 12:7 **really was** a promise to preserve the "poor" mentioned in verse five rather than "the

Is Our English Bible Inspired?

words of the Lord" mentioned in verse six? How can we clear up the confusion brought by an erroneous translation and a phony claim?

The answer is embarrassingly simple **if** the Bible is our **final authority** in **all matters** of faith and practice. All you need to do is read the entire psalm and the answer is clear.

1 Help, LORD; for the godly man ceaseth; for the faithful fail from among the children of men.

2 They **speak** vanity every one with his neighbour: with flattering **lips** and with a double heart do they **speak**.

3 The LORD shall cut off all flattering **lips**, and the **tongue** that **speaketh** proud things:

4 Who have said, With our **tongue** will we prevail; our **lips** are our own: who is lord over us?

5 For the oppression of the poor, for the sighing of the needy, now will I arise, saith the LORD; I will set him in safety from him that puffeth at him.

6 The **words** of the LORD are pure words: as silver tried in a furnace of earth, purified seven times.

7 Thou shalt keep them, O LORD, thou shalt preserve them from this generation for ever.

8 The wicked walk on every side, when the vilest men are exalted.

When you **actually read the Bible**, instead of **thoughtlessly** accepting the vain droning of scholarship, you see that Psalm 12 describes a comparison of the **words** of the Lord versus the **words** of the wicked. The entire psalm is about **words**, not "the poor." In verse two we find three references to words: "speak," "lips," "speak." Verse three contains three more references to words: "flattering lips," "tongue," "speaketh." In verse four the wicked "said" something with their "tongue" and "lips." Finally, after **eight** references to the **words** of the wicked, we have these evil words compared to the "words of the LORD" in verse six.

It is plain to any **honest person** that the subject of the psalm is "words." Why would anyone try to make it "the weak" unless they had a hidden agenda? Maybe someone wanted to eliminate one of the greatest promises of preservation found in the Bible by simply "correcting" the Hebrew with their own private interpretation.

Can the Originals be "corrected? No, **no, NO!** The Originals were perfect, without error when written. But, as we all know, the Originals, both Hebrew and Greek disappeared long ago. Today we have only copies. Some of these copies are better than others, but they are still copies. Within these copies are some errors which **are corrected** by our English Bible. Following are a few examples.

2 Samuel 21:19

> **2 Samuel 21:19** And there was again a battle in Gob with the Philistines, where Elhanan the son of Jaareoregim, a Bethlehemite, slew *the brother of* Goliath the Gittite, the staff of whose spear *was* like a weaver's beam.

First Samuel, chapter seventeen, makes it perfectly clear that **David killed Goliath**. Here in Second Samuel is a record of how Elhanan later killed Goliath's brother. You will note that the words, *"the brother of"* are in italics, meaning they were added by the translators of the King James Bible. Why? There are two reasons:

1. If the words *"the brother of"* are not added to the text, then the verse claims that Elhanan killed **Goliath**, rather

Is Our English Bible Inspired?

than his brother. Such a rendering contradicts the plain evidence of 1 Samuel seventeen where David is credited with killing Goliath. Thus, you produce the "bible" Bible-haters have been looking for for centuries, a "bible" with a contradiction. In fact, the following modern versions contain this "contradiction:" the Revised Standard Version, the American Standard Version, the New American Standard Version, the New International Version, the New Revised Standard Version, the New Century Version, the English Standard Version, the New Century Version and the Living Bible, to name a few. (As weel as the 1599 Geneva Bible.)

To keep from misleading the reader as to who killed Goliath, the King James translators "corrected," not **the Original Hebrew**, but **the Hebrew they HAD** and added *"the brother of"* to the verse. On what authority did they do this? On the authority that 1 Samuel makes it plain that David was the one who killed Goliath.

2. The second authority they used is found right there in the Bible. In 1 Chronicles, chapter twenty, we find the parallel passage to 2 Samuel, chapter twenty-one, where verse five reads:

> **1Chron. 20:5** And there was war again with the Philistines; and Elhanan the son of Jair slew Lahmi the brother of Goliath the Gittite, whose spear staff was like a weaver's beam.

The reader will notice that the phrase, "the brother of" **is not** in italics. That's because **it was not added by the translators**. Why? Because it was in the Hebrew. So, the **second** authority the King James translators had for adding

65

this phrase to 2 Samuel 21 was 1 Chronicles 20. (**That's** an acceptable authority. Isn't it?)

This leads to a second contradiction in those flawed modern versions. Not only do they introduce a contradiction between 1 Samuel seventeen and 2 Samuel twenty-one by deleting *"the brother of,"* but they introduce a **second** contradiction between 2 Samuel twenty-one and 1 Chronicles twenty which plainly states Elhanan didn't kill Goliath, but his brother, Lahmi.

What this means is, **if we had** the Original autograph of 2 Samuel we would find "the brother of" in chapter twenty-one, verse nineteen. Aren't you glad you have a King James Bible which corrected the error in **the Hebrew we have** to preserve the correct reading?

1 John 2:23

1 John 2:23 Whosoever denieth the Son, the same hath not the Father: *[but] he that acknowledgeth the Son hath the Father also.*

We noted in the previous chapter how the second half of this verse is in italics, meaning there is no Greek support for those words in the Textus Receptus. We needn't replow the same ground but will suffice it to say this is another place where **the Greek we have** is corrected by our English Bible. If we had the **Original** autograph for 1 John we would find the words supplied by the King James translators in the text.

No one, except Ken Barker and his NIV translators, believes that **the Originals** can be corrected by the English.

But we do believe God has preserved His infallible text, in spite of a few omissions in the **copies** of Hebrew and Greek that we have.

"The nearer I approach the end of my pilgrimage, the clearer is the evidence of the divine origin of the Bible."

Samuel F. B. Morse

9
That Book in Your Hand

So the question is this: is the King James Bible "inspired" or "preserved?" The answer is simple, **both!** It is not inspired in the same fashion as the Originals were. In the case of the Originals, they started with a blank sheet of paper and when a man was done writing, the result was **the inspired originals**. (Ps.12 :6) We all know the King James translators did not sit in a room with a blank sheet of paper and write as did Isaiah. No, they had both Greek and Hebrew manuscripts, numerous early English translations as well as foreign language translations. For that reason we say the King James Bible is the **preserved** word of God. (Ps. 12:7)

But, is the King James Bible inspired in that it is the preservation of the inspired words of God? Absolutely. As one great preacher asked, "If the King James Bible isn't inspired, at what point did inspiration 'fall out'?"

The Real Test

There are some who, overwhelmed with feelings of inferiority when facing scholarship, will say, "That's exactly what I believe!" That isn't what they believe at all. They are dancing with semantics and hoping no one steps on their toes. Pinning them down takes the same finesse you need in pinning down a Roman Catholic when he claims he's "saved." He wants you to think he's OK, so he gives the right answer but it means something different to him than it does to you. Example:

To a Roman Catholic: "Are you saved?"
Meaning: Have you taken the death, burial & resurrection of Jesus Christ as the sole payment for your sin?

From the Roman Catholic: "Yes."
Meaning: I'm religious and haven't killed anyone so I think I'm safe.

To a Roman Catholic: "Have you accepted Christ?"
Meaning: Have you taken the death, burial & resurrection of Jesus Christ as the sole payment for your sin?

From the Roman Catholic: "Sure."
Meaning: I ate Him yesterday morning at church.

As you can see you can ask the Roman Catholic the right question and get a **right sounding** answer. But there is **one question** that will flush them out.

To a Roman Catholic: "If you died right now **do you know for a fact** that you would go to Heaven?
Meaning: Have you taken the death, burial & resurrection of Jesus Christ as the sole payment for your sin?

Now **that** is the question that will smoke out a Roman Catholic! You now have him over a barrel. If he says "No."

Is Our English Bible Inspired?

he is admitting he's lost. If he says "Yes" then he's **still** going to Hell, for the Roman Catholic Church teaches no one can **know** for a fact they are going to Heaven, and if someone says they are, they are guilty of the "Sin of Presumption" and therefore damned.

This is the same "dance" you get when you ask some men if they believe the Bible. They want you to think they are OK so they will say what you want to hear, but it will mean something different to them than it does to you. Example:

To the Dancer: "Do you believe the Bible?"
Meaning: Do you believe the King James Bible is perfect, without error.

Dancer: "Absolutely."
Meaning: I believe that somewhere two thousand years ago there was a perfect Book somewhere known as "the Originals," but there is no perfect Bible on earth today.

To the Dancer: "Do you believe the King James Bible is the word of God?"
Meaning: Do you believe the King James Bible is perfect, without error.

Dancer: "You better believe it! I would never use one of those modern perversions."
Meaning: I believe that somewhere two thousand years ago there was a perfect Book somewhere known as "the Originals," but there is no perfect Bible on earth today.

As you can see the Dancer parries your every move. But, just like the Roman Catholic, there is one question that will smoke him out.

To the Dancer: "Do you believe **that Book you're holding in your hand** is the perfect, flawless word of God?"
Meaning: Do you believe the King James Bible is perfect, without error.

Dancer: You're a heretic! No translation can be perfect. Only the Originals were perfect.

It's Ridiculous!

I once had an antagonist against the King James Bible tell me, "To believe that **one English translation** is the perfect Word of God is ridiculous!"

I responded, "You're right. Would you believe anything so ridiculous?"

"Never."

"But you believe the Red Sea parted and the Children of Israel crossed on dry ground. You believe that a man walked on top of water. You believe a jackass talked. You believe Jesus raised dead people. You believe that someday you're going to fly through the air without an airplane. Right?"

"Yes."

"**All of those things are ridiculous** but we believe them. Believing the King James Bible is the perfect Word and words of God is truly ridiculous. But it is **way down** on a **long list** of "ridiculous" things we believe."

The Bottom Line

The bottom line is this. The Word of God is **not** some pile of manuscripts that have been lost for thousands of years which we couldn't read if we had them. The Bible isn't the Textus Receptus Greek from which we get our King James Bible. The King James Bible is the Word and words of God and has no errors: not a comma, not a semicolon, not a word. If it could have **one** mistake, it could have **two**, it could have **twenty**, it could have one thousand. But it only needs **one mistake** to cease to be the **perfect, inspired** word of God.

Other Helpful books from:
DayStar Publishing

* A Charted History of the Bible*
By James Kahler. The first book every Christian should have to help them understand how we got our Bible. Easy to read charts with brief, but informative, synopsis on important events in the history of the Bible. $5.95

* Gipp's Understandable History of the Bible *
By Samuel C. Gipp. A thorough study of the history of the Bible with information on King James, the translators, where Bible manuscripts came from, the Greek witnesses and numerous comparisons of various modern versions. $24.95

* Bread of Life *
By Ted Warmack. A wonderfully complete general study of the Bible covering numerous subjects of interest to Christians, both old and new. Workbook sized and easy to read. $17.95

* The Bible Believer's Guide to Dispensationalism *
By David E. Walker. For the student who wants to better understand how to "rightly divide" the Word of truth. $21.95

* Biblical Youth Work *
By Jim Krohn. One of the leading youth men in the country shows how you can have a successful youth work without compromising or dropping your standards. $12.95

* Living With Pain *
By Samuel C. Gipp. Millions live in constant pain everyday. Dr. Gipp, who has suffered a broken neck has lived with daily pain for over three decades. In this book he helps those who are hurting to deal with their pain. $3.95

* Life's Great Moments *

By Jim White. We've all heard of "Murphy's Law." Jim White says, "Murphy was an optimist!" Read about the most amazing and hilarious happenings in this man's life. $8.95

*For His Pleasure *

By Samuel C. Gipp. Ever wonder why God put you on earth? Ever wonder what your purpose for existing is? This book will help you know what you should be doing every single day of your life. A must read for all Christians. $9.95

* Corruptions in the New King James Bible *

By Jack Munday. Many Christians are fooled into thinking the NKJV is a King James Bible without the "thees" and "thous." Jack Munday exposes the drastic changes found in the New King James Version. $7.95

*Basic Bible Doctrines *

By David E. Walker. Two individual volumes to explain what happened to the new Christian when they were saved and to start them in the right direction in their Bible. $7.95 ea.

* Old Paths Preaching Methods *

By James A. Lince. Before he went home to be with the Lord Bro. Lince recorded and published this work which has been a real help to both preachers and Christian. $13.95

* The Answer Book *

By Samuel C. Gipp. This book has become a classic. It answers over 60 charges brought against the King James Bible. In publication for almost two decades it is still in great demand. Nothing in this book has been refuted. $6.95

* In Spirit and in Truth *
By Jeff Williams. This book explains the errors of the Charismatic Movement. In a workbook format with answers to be filled in, this book deals with tongues, healing, signs & wonders and other errors of this movement. $14.95

* Fight On! *
By Samuel C. Gipp. Short, one-page, stories which will encourage the reader to "Fight On!" as others have before them. $24.95

* More Fight On! Stories *
By Samuel C. Gipp. A second volume of the popular **Fight On!** series. 300 more pages of short stories which will encourage the reader to keep going through tough times. $24.95

* The Geneva Bible, the Trojan Horse *
By Samuel C. Gipp. The Geneva Bible, a predecessor of the King James, was a good translation. But it wasn't perfect. Today, in an attempt the pry the King James Bible out of the of Christians and get them to use anything else, an edition called the "1599" is being promoted as superior to the King James Bible. Find out why it isn't. $5.95

* Valiant for the Truth *
A two-year course suitable for Christian schools, home schoolers, Bible institutes, Youth Groups or individuals who simply want to be able to answer those who relentlessly attack the authority of their Bible. Produced in two series', 11 and 12, each series contains twelve lessons that simplify the most difficult answers to questions about the authority of the King James Bible. $59.95 per series

* Rightly Dividing God's Word *

By Victor Shingler. Another look at how to correctly interpret Scripture. $8.95

DayStar also has sermons and lessons on CD and DVD as well as over a dozen posters for teens, youth ministries or just for fun!.

Check out DayStarPublishing.com or call 1-800-311-1823